Barn Roofs,

Quail Coveys,

and General Mischief

By Laurie J. White

As told to her by Alfred W. Jones
(more or less)

Barn Roofs, Quail Coveys, and General Mischief

Library of Congress Control Number: 2010903312

ISBN 978-0-9801877-2-4

The Shorter Word Press
1345 Butler Bridge Road
Covington, GA 30016

www.theshorterword.com

In memory of Pappy

Table of Contents

Chapter 1

The Daisy

I grew up in the early 1900's in Dalton, Georgia. We lived in a painted brick house that's still standing on the northwest corner of Thornton Avenue and Emery Street. That's Emery with an "e," by the way. The street sign says Emory with an "o," as in Emory University, but the sign is wrong.* I'm sure of that because the street is named after Mr. Emery Blunt, the first mayor of Dalton. Back then our house was considered to be out from town, and there was nothing in back of us but miles of woods and open fields. So we boys had plenty of incentive and opportunity to hunt and explore and get into lots of general mischief.

---

* The street sign was finally corrected, but it misspelled the name of the man it was honoring for years.

My mama was Ellen Cabray Wortley from Ypsilanti, Michigan. Back in the early 1900's, she and her father used to travel by train through Georgia on their way to Florida to spend some of the winter in the warmer climate there. They always stopped for a while in Dalton and stayed at the old Hotel Dalton on Hamilton Street. I say "old" because the hotel, along with that whole city block, burned down in 1911. A real disaster. So the hotel standing there today is not the same building, though it's an old one as well. It was during one of Mama's trips through Dalton that she met my father, Walter Jones, a native of Dalton and a lawyer, and they were soon married. After about one year, my brother Clark made his appearance in the world, and with the passing of a couple more years, Walter showed up. I came chasing after Walter just 15 months later, and he and I did practically everything together.

At Christmas Walter and I usually got the same toys, or pairs of things that went together. Not much point in getting just one baseball glove, you see, or getting a baseball bat but no baseball. So we tended to plan together what we should ask Santa for each year. Christmases were much simpler back then, and we only got one or two things.

One particular year, I was the first to broach the subject. "Walter, what should we ask for this Christmas?" It was coming up on Halloween, and I had already begun to calculate what might be most essential for our future explorations and hunting endeavors. Walter was eight, and I was just three months away from turning seven.

"Papa said last Christmas that we were almost old enough for a BB gun," I continued. "Do you think Mama might think that was all right?"

Walter glanced up at me. He and I were squatting behind a huckleberry bush while spying on a rabbit that was eating lettuce in Mama's backyard garden. "I don't know. But if you don't quit talking, that rabbit will run."

"Well, Mama would rather we run it off, anyway."

"Now that's probably true. But we could let the rabbit have its fill and then tell her we could get rid of all the rabbits if we had a BB gun."

That sounded like a plan.

Whether our logic had any effect on Mama, I seriously doubt. Mama usually saw through our ruses, but come Christmas morning of 1915, Walter and I found ourselves in joint custody of a brand new Daisy repeating air rifle. We were elated. We had also gotten some camping gear as gifts that morning, so we put up our tent in the living room and pretended we were on a big hunt. All we needed was something suitable to shoot.

We had our Christmas dinner at noon, and Mama and Papa went upstairs to take an afternoon nap, as was their custom. This was a common practice in the South in those days. It was a warm day for that time of year, and I soon wandered outside to survey the possibilities for testing out our marksmanship. I had just stepped off the back porch when I heard some clucking over toward the side yard. Our neighbor's eight fat hens were perched on a hedge of Carolina jasmine that divided our property from theirs. About that time Walter came out to join me. I didn't have to say a word. All I did was point.

Pop!

The sight of a hen toppling off that hedge was exhilarating.

Pop!

Pop!

We swapped back and forth, taking turns with the gun as we congratulated ourselves on our accurate aim. Walter and I killed all eight of those hens.

In the midst of our mutual bragging, I heard the screen door slap shut, and we turned to see Mama. It only took her a minute to surmise the situation. Then with a very deliberate calmness, she walked over to that hedge and peeked on the other side to confirm what she already suspected. It was while she was walking over there that it began to sink in on both Walter and me that we might possibly have done something catastrophically bad.

My memory of the rest of that Christmas day is hazy, but I don't recollect getting spanked or switched. Mama usually reserved a small hickory branch for when we were deliberately naughty, and that was often enough. However, I will never forget delivering a painful apology to our neighbors, the Alpers. After all, there were no freezers in those days, and no way to preserve all that meat. So the Alpers shared the hens with us and a few other families, but if any meat were left over, it just went to waste. The baked chicken mama fixed was awfully good, but I felt guilty that I was enjoying it so much.

The Alpers had lost not just the meat but the eggs they were getting each morning too. It took Walter and me until the next September to work off our debt to them. We mowed their lawn and did odd jobs around their place and, I might add, didn't have quite as much free time to go hunting with our BB gun. But we did get to keep it.

Chapter 2

The Barn

W hen I was eight years old, Mama and Papa provided us with a new brother, Tom. He was interesting and entertaining to some degree, but Clark, Walter, and I were restless for him to hurry and get big enough to actually do things. Meanwhile, we had to be content just to let him grow. Whenever we were given baby-sitting duty, we did our best to place Tom where he couldn't get hurt or in the way, but where we could still see him as we amused ourselves off to the side. We usually ended up playing a card game or shooting marbles, the latter being somewhat tricky since Tom might put a marble in his mouth and choke if we allowed him to get too close. But we were always careful.

One Saturday Mama and Papa had to go sing at a funeral. They both had nice voices, and they sang duets together sometimes for funerals and weddings. They said they'd be gone around two hours and for the three of us to watch Tom during that time. Tom was about two, and that would make Clark thirteen, Walter eleven, and me ten.

"Who wants to go pull the car around to the back door?" Papa asked as he came down the stairs ready to leave.

"I'll do it!" Clark hollered from the sitting room where he was reading. He was the quickest to speak up, but we all enjoyed driving the car no matter how short the distance. Several years before, Papa had bought us an electric car, and we were, in fact, the first family in Dalton to own one. All three of us could drive it by that time. We had practiced driving around the yard even before we could reach the pedals. In an electric car, you see, you didn't have to shift gears or push a clutch, so one of us could steer while another got down on the floor and operated the accelerator and brake with his hands. Of course, we didn't go out on the road that way, though we were tempted to. No driver's license was needed in those days either, so I started driving out on the road when I was around age twelve.

As Clark pulled up near the back porch steps, Mama turned to Walter and me as we stood in the open doorway. "I know Clark will be careful, but I'm counting on both of you to watch Tom, too. What- ever you do, don't let him out of your sight." Then she got in the car with Papa and waved back at us with a smile.

Soon after they drove off, a friend from down the street showed up at our door with a few other boys. "We were wondering if y'all would like to play some ball?" they asked. We had one of the better places to play in our neck of town.

"Sure!" I said without hesitation.

"But what will we do with Tom?" Clark wanted to know.

"How about tying him into a chair in the yard so he can watch the game? That would keep him content for a spell," I suggested.

"I don't know," Walter countered. "He'd be too close to the game. He could get hit by a fly ball."

There was a moment of silence while we all pondered alternatives. Then Clark had an idea. "Why don't we tie him up on the barn roof? He could see the whole game from up there."

"You know, that just might work," Walter re- sponded thoughtfully. "He'd be too far up to get hit by a fly, and we could still keep an eye on him just like Mama said."

The logic sounded impeccable to me.

Clark and I went directly to the barn to get a ladder while Walter found some rope. Without much more ado than that, Clark hauled little Tom up the ladder with Walter and me climbing right behind. We pulled off a shingle on either side of the ridgeline of the roof. On an old barn that's not hard to do, and split shingles were cheap back then and easy to replace. Papa always had a pile of extras just lying around. We put Tom's legs into the holes. Then reaching through the holes, Clark tied Tom's feet together so he was snug and secure, straddling the ridge and unable to get his legs out and fall. As we climbed back down, Walter said that once the game was underway, Tom would probably enjoy the privilege of his bird's-eye-view seating arrangement.

The game was in full swing with two on base, one out, and it was my turn to bat when Mama and Papa came driving up the driveway. The maddest I ever saw my Mama in my entire life was the moment she spied her baby up on that roof. Of course, Tom immediately started crying the second he saw his mama waiting for him on the ground. I truly don't believe he had so much as whimpered until then.

Papa climbed the ladder to rescue Tom while the neighborhood boys were hustled home. Clark, Walter, and I were sent to our rooms. For a somber hour or so, we waited upstairs in dread of what would surely be a "serious consequence for our reprobate behavior," as Mama put it. That was said in the heat of anger, however, and she and Papa did eventually comprehend that our concern for Tom had been genuine, even if entirely dimwitted.

I don't recall what our punishment was, but it was not so severe as to quash our delight in recounting the event over and over in the years to come. Tom retained no memory of his rooftop experience, and as my own children grew up and heard the story, they suggested that their uncle was too traumatized to recall it. I doubt that, however. After all, he had a ringside seat for the game.

Chapter 3

The Bobwhite

It was a chilly afternoon after school in late November when I walked into Walter's and my bedroom with the BB gun slung over my shoulder. I carefully stood on a chair and hung it up over the doorway. Walter and I had read a story about a cowboy who kept his shotgun over the front door of the house, and we thought that would be a fine place to put our air gun. Papa said our bedroom door would do as well, and so we put some nails in the wall above the door to hold it there.

"Did you try to get a quail with the BB gun? You should know you can't do that." Walter spoke with a slightly condescending tone. He had commenced life in this world merely 15 months before my own birthday, but he continually enjoyed playing the role of the older and wiser big brother.

"No, I was just out looking for squirrels." I was fudging a little on this. I didn't care to feed Walter's sense of superiority by allowing he was right. "Mama is worried a squirrel may have gotten into the attic and built a nest," which was completely true, "and I thought I might help thin out their numbers a bit," which was not a total fib either, though in actuality I had been much more attentive to possible quail habitats than squirrels. I had spied a few bobwhites crossing an open area not 200 yards from the house and tried to shoot one. But Walter was right, of course. It takes a gun with pellets, or shot, fanning out in a pattern to bring down a quail.

"It is quail season though, you know." I spoke as if that fact had just occurred to me as I continued my facade.

"I know."

"Why don't we ask Papa again about taking out the 12-gauge?"

"You can if you want to, Alfred. Last time I asked, though, Papa just laughed. He said he'd just as soon allow it as not, but he reckoned he'd respect Mama's wishes. You know, she's always been determined that we should wait until I hit twelve. So, guess we got another year to go." Walter sounded resigned.

I thought about this for a time, and next day I went to Mama. I had a plan. She was standing over the kitchen table kneading brown bread for supper. I had combed my hair, washed my face and hands, and I stood in the kitchen doorway smiling and said, "Mama, can I help you with anything today?" I tried to sound nonchalant. My excessively polite manner was probably too out of character and raised her suspicions.

Mama glanced up. "You can sweep the kitchen while I finish kneading this bread."

I carefully swept the wood floor and put away the broom. "Is there anything else?"

"Well, the coal bucket needs filling, and then you could add some coal to the fire. We need the house to stay good and warm to help the bread rise," she added with a smile.

So I filled the bucket and stoked the fire, adding coal with the big metal tongs we kept by the fireplace. She thanked me and then pointed to the corner of the room and said it would certainly be nice if I took that clothesbasket upstairs. It was piled full of clean clothes from the clothesline.

When I came back downstairs, Mama was covering the dough to let it rise. She looked up and said, "Now, are you here to ask me about taking the shotgun out?" Mama had seemed to read my mind at times before, but this beat all.

"Yes, ma'am, I am," I confessed. I told her that Walter and I would gladly pledge ourselves to months of extra chores if we just didn't have to suffer the irretrievable loss of another quail season with no appropriate firearm.

"Well, I was planning to tell you and Walter that you could have it this year anyway," and then she added, "but the chores are a fine idea."

I hoped Walter would think so.

Next morning Walter and I were out early with Nell, the neighbor's bird dog. It was a cold, bright Saturday. There were no quail where I spotted them the day before, but we walked on to other low spots that seemed likely settings for a covey to feel secure, all the while hoping that Nell would pick up a scent. Walter took the first turn with the gun because he was older.

Sometimes you have to downright kick up a quail covey to make it fly. You can't shoot them on the ground because you might hit your dog if you are hunting with one. The natural instinct of quail is to hide. They can be visible one minute and then the next just plain disappear. They know how to scurry up under a leaf or branch, and their camouflage is so perfect, you can't see them even when you are certain where they are. But if you keep coming toward them, they get panicked. Then they try to startle you by making a racket and flying up all at once. Soon as they take off, they zoom away really fast, and it's just a matter of seconds before they are out of range, so you have to be quick as you take aim and fire.

Walter and I were having a fine time walking through the leaves on this crisp morning when suddenly Nell froze stiff. She was staring just over to the south end of a dried-up creek bed. Walter inched forward in the direction of Nell's gaze, and he got the shotgun up and ready to aim. As I approached through the tall grass, there came an explosion, and it wasn't from the shotgun. If you've ever heard a quail covey take off, you'll know what I mean. There was this great blast of commotion right in my face, and it was so sudden and so loud, it caught me entirely off guard. However, Walter retained his wits just fine. He fired a shot right into the cloud of feathered prey and got his first quail.

Walter was so excited he wanted to head back home right then, but he stayed out with me just a bit to let me try to shoot a bird of my own. We turned back toward the house though after a spell. When we got home, the whole family was full of congratulations for my brother and his "quick aim" and "natural talent" for hunting. "First time out and he's gotten a quail," each one in turn seemed to exclaim.

We already knew how to dress a bird, so Walter went right to it. In no time at all Mama had it simmering on the stove, and soon it was ready to be served with the rest of our dinner, that is, our midday meal. Walter managed to give us each a bite, though a quail is not much more than just a few bites in itself. As he ate the rest, I could tell he was savoring every morsel.

The next day was Sunday, and Mama and Papa didn't allow us to hunt on Sunday, so I didn't even ask. I knew if I sneaked out early, I could shoot a bird and be back in plenty of time to clean up and get dressed before the morning service at First Presbyterian, but all I did was to lie in bed imagining it for a bit. It seemed like a long afternoon after we got home from church. I mostly spent the time reading a book for school and then playing some catch with Walter. Papa didn't object to that as long as we were quiet. It would have been a pleasant day under other circumstances, but all the while I couldn't quit thinking about how Walter had shot a quail and I hadn't.

Then Monday came, and I had to go to school. It wasn't but a few blocks down Thornton Avenue to City Park School, and Walter and I always walked, as did all of the children back then. As soon as we met up with some of the other fellows in our grade, Walter began recounting Saturday's adventure. I suppose I wasn't too keen on hearing the story again, so I trudged on into my classroom. Our first period began, and it was hard to stay focused on the lessons. After an hour or so, I approached my teacher, Mrs. Grace Flemister. "Mrs. Flemister, I'm not feeling too well."

"Well, Alfred, I thought you looked a little distracted this morning. You don't feel hot," she said as she put her hand to my forehead, "but you may be coming down with something. Can you walk home all right?"

"Yes, ma'am. I believe I can."

"Well then, maybe you should run along and let your mama look after you."

And so I did.

When I came in the back door of the house, Mama didn't say a word. But there on the chair in the hall lay my hunting coat, my britches, my boots, and the shotgun with some shells. And she'd even tied Nell to a post on the back porch. This time Mama had gone way beyond telepathy. I think she knew what I was going to do before I even knew it. I changed my clothes and took off to the woods. I killed my first quail that afternoon.

But that's not quite the end. I did in fact kill two birds that afternoon, and after congratulating me, Mama hurried me up telling me to clean and dress them soon as I could. Then she cooked them and made the most delicious looking gravy. Even so, I never got to taste it nor the birds. Instead, I soon found myself walking to Mrs. Flemister's house with instructions to present my prize quails to her along with an honest confession. I took my time getting there.

As it turned out, the experience was not so dreadful after all. Mama had already told Mrs. Flemister everything, and after listening to my follow-up apology, my teacher seemed delighted to get such a delicious treat for supper. She graciously thanked me and even remarked on my obvious abilities as a hunter.

Walter was going to tease me about the fact that I had not gotten to eat my own quail. But secretly I savored the flavor of having my small deception at school resolved, and though I would never have admitted it to another living soul, the pleased look in the eyes of my teacher had been a sweet reward.

History Tidbits

Get this COWBOY CARBINE with your CHRISTMAS MONEY
Like Bill Got His!
GOLDEN-BANDED 1000-SHOT
RED RYDER cowboy CARBINE
FREE CATALOG
DAISY AIR RIFLES
only $2.95
DAISY MANUFACTURING COMPANY, PLYMOUTH, MICHIGAN, U. S. A.

The BB Gun

Air-powered guns have been around longer than most people think. In fact, Lewis and Clark carried an early model air rifle on their historic expedition in 1804. But contrary to what some people think, these early air rifles were very different from a BB gun. These original air rifles fired large caliber bullets or balls, not small BB's, and they had the same force as a rifle that used gunpowder. Another difference is that the BB gun is a *gun* not a rifle, that is, it has no rifling inside the barrel (spiraling grooves that give the bullet a spin so it will fly straighter). Also, the early air rifles were rare and expensive. In contrast, the BB gun was and still is relatively cheap, and though certainly not a toy, it is also not on the level of a serious firearm, making it perfect for a young person who isn't ready for a full-fledged rifle or shotgun yet. Air rifles began in Europe with the earliest known model dating back to 1580. But the amazingly popular BB gun, which came along just over a hundred years ago, has a unique American story all its own.

In the late 1800's, Clarence Hamilton was working in Plymouth, Michigan, for the Plymouth Iron Windmill Company, a company that was not doing so well. No one seemed to be buying windmills. Then in 1886 Clarence had an idea for helping the company sell windmills. After months of tinkering with various designs, he invented a novelty gun with a small lead pellet propelled by compressed air for the company to use as a gift to farmers whenever they bought a windmill. When the president of the company saw the gun and fired it for the first time, he reportedly exclaimed, "Boy, that's a daisy!" and the name stuck.

At first the Daisy BB gun was used to encourage the sales of the windmills, just as Clarence had intended. But people liked the guns so much, the windmill company decided to begin selling the guns as a separate product. Soon the Daisy air gun was outselling the windmills! Eventually, the company discontinued the windmills altogether and changed its name to the Daisy Manufacturing Company. It has been successfully selling BB guns ever since.

Then in 1914 a man named Charles Lefevre took the BB gun to a whole new level when he devised a pump-style BB gun with repeating action and manufactured it with Daisy. It was probably this new pump gun that Walter and Alfred got for Christmas.

Daisy's most famous BB gun so far is the Red Ryder Air Rifle (called a "rifle" even though it has a smooth-bore barrel). It came out in 1936 and was later featured in the movie classic *A Christmas Story.*

Refrigerators and Freezers

In 1915, around the time when Alfred and Walter shot the chickens, neither they nor their neighbors had any means of preserving the meat from the dead hens beyond just a few days. In fact, the electric refrigerator was just being invented at that particular time, and only the extremely wealthy had one. Most homes were equipped instead with the non-electric counterpart to a refrigerator, an icebox.

An icebox was an insulated wood or enameled cabinet that held a huge block of ice in an upper compartment. A cubic foot of ice weighs around 60 pounds, and most people got their blocks in 25, 50, or 75 pound blocks. That should give you some idea of the size of these giant ice cubes. Each week the iceman would come to one's neighborhood and go from door to door delivering fresh "cakes" of ice, as the big blocks were called. Using enormous tongs, he placed the ice in the ice compartment with a water tray positioned underneath to catch the drips as the ice slowly melted during the week.

An incredibly modern convenience in its own day, the icebox kept food at refrigerator temperatures right in the kitchen close at hand. There was no longer any need to haul up a bucket with your milk in it from the bottom of a well or spring, and meat and vegetables could be kept fresh for several days.

The first motorized refrigerators for home use came out in 1915, but these first models, as with all new technology, were too pricey for regular people to buy. Then in 1923, Frigidaire introduced the first self-contained refrigeration unit with the motor and the compressor in the same housing as the icebox itself, and its price was much more affordable. It had a freezer compartment roomy enough to hold two ice trays. Buyers were thrilled! They could produce their own ice at home for the first time in history.

As new refrigerator models were introduced during the 1920's and 30's, the freezer compartment became larger. That's when preserving food at home by way of freezing finally became an option, and mischievously murdered hens forever after could be preserved.

Marbles

What did little boys do before Nintendo? Lots of things, for sure, but one activity that remained wildly popular up until the 1950's was shooting marbles, a highly competitive, entertaining pastime that could be played almost anywhere at anytime if you just had your bag of marbles with you.

These little round balls derive their name from one of the materials that is sometimes used to make them, that is, marble. However, marble marbles are pricey, and most marbles are made from cheaper materials such as clay or glass.

Marbles go way back in history. We know the ancient Romans played marbles because games with marbles are mentioned often in Roman letters and journals. Emperor Caesar Augustus, who reigned at the time of Christ, played games with marbles made of nuts that were sanded and rounded down. Archaeologists have found marbles everywhere from the Mississippian earth mounds of Native American tribes, to the 4000-year-old Minoan sites on the island of Crete. Marbles have even been found in ancient Egyptian tombs. In fact, shooting marbles may be one of the oldest games on earth.

Marbles were handmade until around 1890 when the first machines were invented to manufacture them. Glass was the easiest material to use to produce machine-made marbles, so that's why glass marbles are the cheapest and most common marbles available to us today. Glass marbles vary in their appearance depending on whether they are painted or glazed with colors, or whether they have colored glass injected into them to form various shapes and designs inside. Each type of design and color has its own special name. On the old TV game show *The 64,000 Dollar Question*, James Crawford won the grand prize one week when he correctly answered the question: "What do turtles, pearls, onionskins, bumblebees, sulphides and chinas have in common?" And what was the winning answer? They are all types of children's marbles.

Alfred and Walter were not allowed to gamble with money, but they considered it fair game if you played "for keeps" with the marbles themselves. So when you knocked an opponent's marble out of the circle, you got to keep it. But because this was really still a type of betting, their mama frowned upon it, and you can be sure no game of marbles was ever played on Sunday. At least not one she knew of. And probably some boys went a little crazy when they gambled away all their marbles, and thus if someone asks you if you've "lost your marbles," they mean, "Have you gone crazy?" So, try not to lose your marbles.

Electric Cars

During Alfred and Walter's early childhood, automobiles were on the road along with horses and wagons. Many of the horse owners complained about the cars spooking their horses, especially the gasoline-powered cars because they were so loud. But most people were excited about these new-fangled contraptions and wanted one of their own as soon as they could afford it. Also, the automobile was seen as the very thing that was going to *clean up* American cities! That may be hard to believe since cars are a major cause of air pollution today, but a very different kind of pollution was threatening the health and sanitation of cities in pre-auto days.

In his article "From Horse Power to Horse-power," Eric Morris explains what a mammoth task it was to keep a horse-driven city like New York City clean:

- 3 to 4 million pounds of manure had to be cleared away each day
- 40,000 gallons of urine had to be disposed of each day
- 15,000 dead horses had to be carted off each year

Most amazing of all, the percentage of fatalities from horses in the year 1900 was higher than today's fatality rate from automobiles! So most folks thought that the car would be the perfect solution—the streets would be both safer as well as much cleaner without all those frisky horses and the waste they produced.

When Alfred's mother and father bought their electric car, there were actually three types of automobiles from which to choose. Each type was powered by something different—steam, gasoline, or electricity. For a while, no one knew for sure which type would win out and take over the market. Steam cars were heavy and slow but were the first to be invented, so there were more of them at first. But by 1910, the race had narrowed down to the electric car and the gasoline car.

The electric car had some major advantages. For one thing, there weren't many gasoline stations around yet, so it was actually easier to find a place to recharge the batteries of your electric car than to find a place to get gas. In addition, you could simply turn on an electric motor with little manual effort at all. In contrast, the gasoline engine had to be hand cranked in order to start. The electric motor was much quieter too than gasoline-powered cars, and there was no gasoline smell. Then, on top of these reasons, you had to learn how to shift gears and use a clutch in a gasoline-powered auto, both of which were unnecessary in an electric car. Thus, it looked as if the electric car would certainly win out. Yet we know it didn't... so what happened?

First of all, an automatic starter was invented for the gasoline car—no more hand cranking to get it going. But, in the end, the factor that really tipped the scales toward gasoline power was speed. As cars became more popular and affordable, roads were improved for their use. Smoother roads meant you could go faster, and people were not just doodling around town anymore but driving from one city to the other much more often. The gasoline car could go both faster and farther without stopping to fill up or re-charge. It was at that point that gasoline cars began to take over the market. Pretty soon, people were not buying any other kind, so manufacturers quit making electric cars—until today, that is.

With soaring gas prices and our modern-day struggle against air pollution, the electric car is making a comeback. New, more advanced models have been developed that go just as fast as gasoline cars. Some of these new electric cars are totally electric, and some are hybrids that run on either electricity or gasoline, so you can switch if you need to.

Who knows? Gas stations might become a thing of the past. Instead, we will have recharging stations to power up our batteries. Soon we may be riding along with quieter engines and, best of all, cleaner air to breathe. However, we shouldn't forget the days of the horse. The next time you hear someone complaining about gasoline engines causing air-pollution, tell them to just be thankful they aren't shoveling manure!

Thomas Edison standing beside a 1914 Detroit Electric

The Bobwhite Quail

The bobwhite quail is the best-known and most hunted species of quail in the United States. There are five other species of quail in our country, but they are only found in the western states. If you're hunting quail in Georgia, you're looking for bobwhites.

Quail season was not regulated by law back in 1919 when Alfred and Walter were hunting in back of their house. Still, the boys had to wait to go hunting until quail were "in season," basically from November to April when quail gather in coveys of anywhere from 5 to 30 birds. In mid-April mating season begins and the coveys break up, not to re-form until October. Quail are harder to hunt if they are not in coveys, so April marks the close of quail season. But even when they are in season, quail are so well camouflaged that they are almost impossible to spot without a good bird dog like Nell.

My dad, Alfred, used to hunt doves as well as quail, so I grew up eating both of these birds occasionally. But I always liked the taste of quail better. Doves are a little smaller so you get even less meat per bird, and also they fly longer distances, which makes their meat darker. Quail meat is somewhat dark when compared to chicken, but it is lighter and tastier than dove.

The bobwhite quail derives its name from its distinctive and easily recognized whistle— "bob-white!" or, "bob-bob-white!" Because the bobwhite's voice is easy to pick out from among other bird songs, it is often the first birdcall a Southern child learns to identify.

If you're not sure what a bobwhite sounds like, you can listen to a recording on this website:

www.dovehunt.com/wave/bobwhite1.wav

Britches and Knickers

My dad called all his pants britches and correctly so. Britches is a term for men's pants that goes back for centuries. However, fashions have greatly changed and men's pants used to come only just past the knee. Many folks think that the word britches refers to knee-pants, but that isn't actually so. When long pants came in, people needed a new term to designate the difference, so knee-pants became known as knickers, and the term britches was still often used to refer to pants of any length.

The word knickers is slang today for underwear, but in the early 1900's, these were boys' pants that buttoned or buckled at the calf, while loose and blousy above. If you look at the cover photo of the four Jones boys, you'll notice that only Clark, standing at far left, has on long pants, a sign that he was older. Tom, on the far right, has on what seems to be a version of short pants more like our modern shorts. It's hard to tell what the two middle boys, Walter and Alfred, have on, but it's either very blousy knickers or shorts.

The word britches is a variation of a much older word—*breeches*. When the term breeches is used, people almost always mean knee-pants, or knickers. Check out the picture from 1789 on the next page. These breeches are fitted and tight all over, and they were worn by both grown men and boys. Then in the next picture, you see a modern-day jockey who is also wearing breeches or knickers. Horseback riding is one place where knee-pants have remained in style. You can probably think of other sports where the players wear knickers because knee-length protection suits the activity.

Gentleman's breeches with silk stockings, 1789

A modern jockey wearing breeches—

Horseback riding is one place where breeches are still in fashion.

Mr. Emery (with an e) Blunt

Ainsworth Emery Blunt was the first mayor of Dalton, but he was not a native Southerner. He was born and raised in New Hampshire. When he was a young man, he felt that God was calling him to ministry, and at the age of 22, he left friends and family to head south to do mission work among the Cherokee tribes who were living in Tennessee and North Georgia. Blunt served as a mechanic and farmer, helping the native people in their struggle to become more "civilized" and to gain acceptance as equals among the white population. He met and married fellow mission worker Harriet Ellsworth, and together they served first in Brainerd, Tennessee, and next at a mission called Candy Creek. Then for the Cherokee people there came a terrible change in fortune.

Before there was ever a gold rush in California, there was a small but significant gold rush in Georgia. Gold was discovered in the foothills of the Appalachian Mountains near Dahlonega, a town named from the Cherokee word "tah-lo-nee-gee," which means yellow rock, or gold. The year was 1828, and it was the first major gold rush in the United States.

White people had already been pushing to get their hands on what remained of Native American lands in the South. Now with the discovery of gold, the mood among whites became frantic to take hold of Cherokee lands in North Georgia. The pressure on the U.S. Congress steadily grew to "do something about those Indians."

Finally, in 1830 Congress passed the Indian Removal Act. The bill would force all Native American tribes still living east of the Mississippi River to move to western territories. President Andrew Jackson signed the bill, and thus began one of the most regrettable and degrading chapters in U.S. history.

One after the other, each of the remaining Southern tribes were forced to leave their native homelands. The Cherokee Nation was the last to go. In the summer of 1838 around 13,000 Cherokees were rounded up at gunpoint from their homes and herded into concentration camps for several months. Many died from dysentery and disease in the hot, cramped quarters. They were then forced to begin the arduous task of walking all the way to Oklahoma on what has become known as the Trail of Tears. They walked all winter. By the end of the journey one-third of the people had perished.

Soldiers were assigned to go along on the journey and make sure no one escaped, and a few other white people voluntarily accompanied the

Cherokees on this hard trek in order to give encouragement and support. Emery Blunt was among them. After several months he became so ill he could not continue and was forced to rejoin his wife and children back in Georgia. They settled down in a small place called Cross Plains. Then in 1847 Cross Plains was incorporated, and the name was changed to Dalton. "Incorporated" means that a town has been given a charter by the state to be an official township and to establish its own town government. Thus, because of its new status as an officially functioning town, Dalton needed a mayor. Mr. Blunt became the first mayor of Dalton. He was also, by the way, the founder of Dalton's First Presbyterian Church.

The Blunt House was built by Emery Blunt in 1848 and is the second oldest house in Dalton. Fully restored, it stands at 506 South Thornton Avenue and is on the National Registry of Historic Places.

The Four Jones Boys

The Jones boys grew up just three doors down from the Blunt house on South Thornton Avenue. They survived the mischievous and occasionally dangerous shenanigans of their early years and made it through high school, only 11 grades back then. All four went initially to Georgia Tech. Clark and Tom both graduated from Tech. Walter transferred to Emory and finished there. My dad, Alfred, was the only one who did not graduate from college. He attended Tech for two years, which brought him smack up to 1929, the infamous year in American history when the Great Depression hit. Finances became extra tight for everyone, and to top it off, Alfred's father was losing his eyesight. His dad had finally been forced to quit his law practice and start a new business. So Alfred returned home to Dalton to help his dad run the new enterprise, Jones Garage, an auto repair shop and wrecker service.

All the boys ended up back in Dalton to live. Clark eventually started his own business, Dalton Public Service, a company that continues to this day under the name of Dalton Service. It is run now by his grandson. Walter landed a job with First National Bank of Dalton and worked his way up to vice president. Tom sold John Deere tractors for a while, served stateside in the Army during World War II, then co-founded J & J Rugs, now J & J

Industries. Alfred sold cars and then worked as a realtor, eventually starting his own company, Jones Real Estate. They all went to First Presbyterian Church and served as elders, except my dad. He said you had to pray better than he did to be an elder, and he remained a life-long deacon.

My dad used to like to say that until he was fifty years old, he had never lived more than a block away from the place where he was born, except for a week he spent in Florida trying to sell used trucks.

Acknowledgements

First, thank you to Anne Dicks, my friend and editor, who has an eagle eye and catches things I would never notice.

Then thank you to all my wonderful and copious cousins who were my inspiration to write this down. I especially hope the young ones will enjoy the stories. Special thanks to cousins Anne Sims, Ellen Tenney, Trisha Bethel, Rosy Haines, Walter Jones, Cathy Rauschenberg, and to my sisters Henrietta Turley and Fran Lewis, all of whom helped me with some of the finer details—especially how they tied Tom to the roof. I went with Trisha's version, by the way. Should we take a family vote to see who agrees?

I was glad I ran this by my brother-in-law Comer Turley, too. He was the only one who knew Daddy had to give up his first quail and take them to Mrs. Flemister for supper. Also, Comer helped me with specifics on quail hunting. You'd think after all those years being around my dad, I'd have known more than I did about quail hunting as well as other things. But your parents die, and *then* you think of all the questions you forgot to ask.

About the Author

I grew up in Dalton on Thornton Avenue just one block south from where my dad Alfred grew up and about a 15-minute walk from City Park and Dalton High where I attended school. I had the same first grade teacher as my dad, though he was 41 years older than I. Changes don't seem to occur quite so rapidly in a small town.

I live now in Covington, Georgia, where I teach history and write materials and books for students from elementary through high school, but I come back to Dalton frequently to visit friends and family. In so many ways, Dalton will always be home.

Laurie Jones White

Other Books by Laurie J. White:

Baktar, A Tale From the Andes
Historical fiction for grades 3-6

*King Alfred's English, A History of the Language
We Speak and Why We Should Be Glad We Do*
A history of English for ages 12 through adult

Free supplemental material for teachers and students is available for all of Laurie White's books. Just go to her website—

www.lauriejwhite.com

www.ingramcontent.com/pod-product-compliance
Lightning Source LLC
Chambersburg PA
CBHW021224020426
42331CB00003B/462